Setting The
Captives Free

By BOB BUESS

Price $1.50
Send 50¢ postage for first 3 books ordered.
Add 5¢ for each additional book.
Texas residents include 4% sales tax.
Individuals may deduct a 35% discount in orders of 30 books or more. Texas residents please include sales tax after the discount is figured.
Discounts do not apply to sets.

Order books from
BOB BUESS
Box 959   •   Van, Texas 75790
Copyright 1975
ISBN 0-934244-02-2

Chapter 1

INTRODUCTION

Lk. 4:18. The Spirit of the Lord is upon me, because he hath anointed me to preach the gospel to the poor; he hath sent me to heal the broken hearted, to preach deliverance to the captives, and recovering of sight to the blind, to set at liberty them that are bruised.

This is the ministry that Jesus gave the church. He declared in Jn. 14:12 that we are to do the same works that He did. Everywhere that Jesus went, He set the captives free.

It is now time for the true believers to come forth and take dominion over Satanic invasions in this world.

Untold numbers within our fellowships are bound by oppressing forces. They need deliverance. Jesus has it for them today.

Much of the sickness, abnormal attitudes, nervousness, poverty, fear, etc., are Satanic forces turned loose upon the individual. The blood washed believer is no exception.

Satan gains entrance through one's will being yielded to him. Rom. 6:16, "Know ye not, that to whom ye yield yourselves servants to obey, his servants ye are to whom ye obey..."

Being saved, or having had a personal encounter with Jesus, does not destroy the will. We can still yield to good or bad.

SATAN DESIRES WORSHIP

Mt. 4:9. All these things will I give thee, if thou wilt fall down and worship me.
Deut. 32:17. They sacrificed unto devils, not to God...
2 Chr. 11:15. He ordained him priests for the high places, and for the devils...
Ps. 106:37. Yea, they sacrificed their sons and their daughters unto devils.
Rev. 13:4. They worshipped the dragon which gave power unto the beast...

Satan has always wanted to be like God. He wants your devotion. He wants your personality yielded over to his will.

He came openly and boldly to Christ desiring full worship.

In the above scriptures we notice that they openly worshipped the Devil.

Satan wants you. If he can't do it openly, then he will try to do it through your besetting sins, sins that you do not recognize to be Satanic. He is subtle.

Yielding to sin is yielding to Satan. As one yields to sin, Satan is allowed to flow through that portion yielded over to him. Satan is dominating or possessing that portion of his life at that time. As one constantly repeats a particular sin, then Satan takes up his abode. As this happens, then the individual is possessed or oppressed in the area that was yielded to Satan.

SATANIC ACTIVITY TO BE STRONG IN THE END TIME

1 Tim. 4:1. Now the Spirit speaketh expressly, that in the latter times some shall depart from the faith, giving heed to seducing spirits, and doctrines of devils.

2 Thes. 2:3-4. Let no man deceive you by any means: for that day shall not come, except there come a falling away first, and that man of sin be revealed, the son of perdition; who opposeth and exalteth himself above all that is called God, or that is worshipped; so that he as God sitteth in the temple of God, shewing himself that he is God.

Acts 20:29. For I know this, that after my departing shall grievous wolves enter in among you, not sparing the flock.

Satan will take just as much as you will yield to him. In some instances he draws an entire church or prayer group into his complete control.

This subtle and seducing spirit will cause good men to read things into the Word that violate the basic teachings of the Word. He conditions you to accept any "wild" idea that he might suggest.

Through his cunning and subtle guidance he gains one area of your life after another until he has complete control. This is happening in our churches today. At one time they were full of

3

revival and the power of God. Then step by step, Satan has entered and gained control. Now many churches are without the power of God that they once knew.

Cults, witchcraft, and spiritualism are gaining much renown in this day and time, a sure sign of the end time. Do not be fooled. These are Satanic powers designed to draw you away from the true supernatural power. These are conditioning the world for the coming of the son of perdition, the antichrist, who will set himself up as god.

The Bible, in the Old Testament, dealt severely with witches and such like. Ex. 22:18, "Thou shalt not suffer a witch to live."

Chapter 2

CHRISTIANS CAN HAVE SATANIC ACTIVITY WITHIN THEIR OWN LIVES

James 4:5. Do ye think that the scripture saith in vain, The spirit that dwelleth in us lusteth to envy?

It is perfectly obvious that this is talking about evil forces working within the Christian. Verse 7, speaking of the same situation, deals with this evil power working within the Christian by saying, "Resist the devil, and he will flee from you."

Luke 13:16. And ought not this woman, being a daughter of Abraham, whom Satan hath bound, lo, these eighteen years, be loosed from this bond...

Jesus called her a daughter of Abraham. She was not called a child of Belial or Satan; however, Satan had bound her with stiffness for eighteen years.

I have seen Jesus set many free from this upon rebuking and casting out this spirit. Many times there have been physical evidences of this spirit leaving the body by screaming, or loud cries, and/or foaming at the mouth.

God sends us to set the captives free.

Mt. 16:22. Then Peter took him, and began to rebuke him. 23. But he turned, and said unto Peter, Get thee behind me, Satan:...

5

In verse seventeen, just prior to this passage, Peter moved by the Holy Spirit and made a profound confession that Jesus was the very Christ.

Now at this point, just a few verses later, Peter yields over to demonic powers to such an extent that his voice is under complete control of the devil. He violently rebuked Jesus. Jesus called it for what it really was, "Get thee behind me, Satan :..."

Ep. 4:25-27. Wherefore putting away lying, speak every man truth with his neighbor : for we are members one of another. Be ye angry, and sin not: let not the sun go down upon your wrath : Neither give place to the devil.

Here the scripture teaches that lying and anger are works of the devil. These were spirit filled believers; yet Paul had to exhort them: "Put off concerning the former conversation of the old man." Verse 22. Satan, through these attitudes, was working his way slowly into their lives. So Paul commanded: "Neither give place to the devil."

Yielding to anger and other activities of the flesh is yielding to satanic forces.

1 Thes. 5:23. And the very God of peace sanctify you wholly; and I pray God your whole spirit and soul and body be preserved blameless unto the coming of our Lord Jesus Christ.

We are to be sanctified wholly. This leads us to understand than there are parts of our lives not yet completely sanctified. What keeps us from being absolutely perfect? Nothing less than satanic activities deeply rooted in us.

Many Christians stop smoking, etc., immediately upon getting converted. Others struggle to break these spirit habits for months and sometimes even years after salvation. Coming to a knowledge of Jesus Christ as personal saviour does not necessarily drive out all evil spirits from your body.

This is what Paul meant when he exhorted the saints in 1 Cor. 6:19-20: "What? Know ye not that your body is the temple of the Holy Ghost which is in you, which ye have of God, and ye are not your own? For ye are bought with a price: therefore glorify God in your body, and in your spirit, which are God's."

Upon reading chapters 5 and 6 of First Corinthians you will see that these were Christians, yet they were guilty of many sins. So in essence Paul said, "Shame on you. Don't you know you belong to Jesus? Glorify God in the body as well as the spirit. Get wrong attitudes out of your body also." In fact, he told them to turn one extreme case over to Satan for the destruction of the flesh in order that his spirit might be saved. 1 Cor. 5:5.

A study of Acts 5 will reveal that Ananias and Sapphira were in all probability spirit filled believers in the Jerusalem church. They loved God enough to sell their property intending to give it to the church. A spirit of covetousness entered when they saw all the money. Then a spirit of lying entered. They lied to Peter on the amount that they had received for the property. Then judgment fell from God upon them for this. Your judgment may not fall as quickly, but you cannot yield to demonic forces and get away with it for long. Satan is a killer. John 10:10 teaches that the enemy is come to steal, kill, and destroy.

Chapter 3

HOW SATANIC FORCES
ENTER THE INDIVIDUAL

SATANIC FORCES ENTER THROUGH FLESHLY ACTIVITIES

Rom. 6:16. Know ye not, that to whom ye yield yourselves servants to obey, his servants ye are to whom ye obey...

2 Pet. 2:19. For of whom a man is overcome, of the same is he brought in bondage.

Even Christians can yield themselves over to satanic forces. God does not destroy the will of man. Man can will to sin or serve God. Satan enters through your carnal will.

Satan soon dominates the area of your life which you yield to him.

That is why dope, alcohol, cigarettes, etc., have such a strong hold. The individual has given Satan legal right to that area of his life.

If you continue to yield anger and such like, you are soon dominated by the spirit of anger. This is Satan.

1 Jn. 2:15-16. Love not the world, neither the things that are in the world. If any man love the world, the love of the Father is not in him. For all that is in the world, the lust of the flesh, and the lust of the eyes, and the pride of life, is not of the Father, but is of the world.

Lust and pride are of the world. Satan is the prince and power of this world. So as you yield to these activities, you are opening your life to the entrance of demonic forces.

We have seen people gloriously liberated from these above mentioned spirits.

Do not entertain any abnormal spirit, or they will soon dominate you.

Gal. 5:19-21. Now the works of the flesh are manifest, which are these: Adultery, fornication, uncleanness, lasciviousness, idolatry, witchcraft, hatred, variance, emulations, wrath, strife, seditions, heresies, envyings, murders, drunkenness, revelings, and such like...

Often we think of the flesh as "poor little ole innocent me;" however, fleshly activities are demon activities in your body. A quick survey of those mentioned above will show you that this is true. Witchcraft is turning to a demon spirit for information rather that the Lord. Heresy is error in teaching which is none other than demonic invasion into your doctrine. Idolatry is direct demon worship or turning from God to the false. So we can deduct that all the others mentioned above are also of the devil.

Rom. 8:6. For to be carnally minded is death... Rom. 8:7. The carnal mind is enmity against God: for it is not subject to the law of God, neither indeed can be.

Normal activity of the flesh is ordained of God. Eating is of God. Gluttony is satanic. Activities of the flesh are described as bringing forth fruit unto death. The fleshly mind is satanic. It is an enemy of God.

We are made up of body, soul, and spirit. Frequently Satan enters through abnormal fleshly activities (such as extreme emotions,

9

abnormal sex, or lust), hate, pride, self-pity, worry, etc.

After he gains control of your flesh, then he moves to completely dominate the mind and finally the spirit.

SATAN ENTERS THROUGH REBELLIOUS ATTITUDES

1 Sam. 15:23. For rebellion is as the sin of witchcraft, and stubbornness is as iniquity and idolatry...

Rebellion and stubbornness are equal to witchcraft and idol worship. As you yield to these forces you are yielding to demons.

Many children rebel against their parents and become sex perverts. With rebellion comes hate. Hate for the parent causes, in some cases, a complete reversal of sex.

This same rebellion and hate for parents is later transferred to rebellion against any form of authority. In the case of a woman she may later rebel against her husband.

Many times hate, rebellion, etc., are manifested before the children by the parents. Then the children pick them up and sooner or later begin to manifest similar attitudes.

Many times, as time passes by, infirm spirits join these spirits.

Many receive deliverance from this stubborn rebellious spirit. We saw the Lord deliver one man who would come home and literally throw his wife around and beat her; then he would repent later and beg forgiveness. He had a stubborn, mean, rebellious spirit.

One lady had such a rebellious anger spirit

for her children that she would fly into a rage at the least offense. Her children were nervous wrecks. God instantly set her free in Jesus' name. She felt the demons come out like long snakes. Then she got down before her children and repented. Many need deliverance from this spirit.

Some children have such hang-ups that they do the opposite of their parents' wishes. This is a rebellious spirit. Usually parent and child both need deliverance.

SATAN CAN ENTER THROUGH ABNORMAL SEX ACTIVITY

Many people, even church leaders, come to me with problems in these areas. One person could not visit without his wife due to the spirit of lust. Another person could not teach as this spirit would hit him and cause him to stagger, become awkward, stammer, etc. Upon deliverance God gave his church a great revival. The spirit entered during his teenage life.

There are many varying degrees of abnormal sex - masturbation, homosexuality, lust, etc. When Satan dominates strongly in these areas, there is no normal marriage life.

Maladjustment, as children, many times causes these problems. Marriage to a perverted person brings one into partial or complete bondage, also. Failure on the part of one mate in his or her marriage vows can cause abnormal responses.

Genuine repentance and forgiveness will destroy any problem if the person truly desires deliverance. In cases of married couples, the offended and the offender must both forgive. I know of a wife who broke her marriage vows. She later returned to her husband. The husband would not forgive her. The results of this unforgiving spirit brought death to their marriage. Even though they lived together in the same house, slept in the same bed, the husband refused to touch his wife in any normal marriage union.

SATAN ENTERS THROUGH THE FAMILY LINE

Sickness, nervousness, fear, and many other abnormal attitudes can be handed down through the family line. Perhaps this is what the Word is teaching when it speaks of the iniquity of the parents passing on to the children to the fourth generation.

Also the parent, especially the father, can open up the family to problems. Usually parents with many problems have children with many problems. Usually, when the parents get deliverance, almost overnight (in case of small children) the children cease having trouble.

SATAN ENTERS THROUGH CRITICAL SPIRITS

Ps. 101:5. Whoso privily slandereth his neighbor, him will I cut off...
2 Tim. 2:16-17. Shun profane and vain babblings: for they will increase unto more ungodliness. And their word will eat as doth a canker...
Mt. 7:1-2. Judge not, that ye be not judged. For

with what judgment ye judge, ye shall be judged: and with what measure ye mete, it shall be measured to you again.

Rom. 12:17 and 19. Recompense to no man evil for evil... Avenge not yourselves, but rather give place unto wrath: for it is written, Vengeance is mine; I will repay, saith the Lord.

"Him will I cut off." Privily slandering our fellow man cuts us off from God's blessings and leaves us open to Satan. "Their word will eat." Vain babblings and gossip and critical spirits will eat and produce ulcers and/or cancer. We are not teaching that all these sicknesses come from critical spirits. We are listing an obvious source of many of our problems.

A mean critical spirit can also produce heart trouble and arthritis. Other negative areas cause similar invasion from Satan.

Some have a negative and critical spirit and do not realize it or do not wish to acknowlege it. I was praying for a woman with this spirit who would not acknowledge it. The spirit would move up to her throat but would not leave. Three different times I asked her if she had a critical spirit. She refused to acknowledge it each time. Then upon asking her again, she began to weep and cry and confess. Instantly she was free. Jesus sends us to "Set the Captives Free".

SATAN ENTERS THROUGH WORRY SPIRITS

"Commit thy way unto the Lord; trust also in him; and he shall bring it to pass. Ps. 37:5. Worry demands that you handle it yourself rather than

13

trusting the Lord. The alcoholic has many problems. He seeks release in the bottle. The negative person has many problems; so he seeks release in the spirit of worry. Both are demonic spirits. Both are from hell. Both are destructive. Worry brings on premature death and sickness as certainly as any other spirit.

Some folks are very religious and would not think of getting drunk, yet they take their "lovely worry spirit" to church, and saints and preachers, in many cases, don't bother to get them delivered. The worry spirit can be just as destructive as the alcoholic spirit; however, it can thrive in many religious atmospheres very nicely.

SATAN ENTERS THROUGH LAZINESS

Pr. 15:19. The way of the slothful man is as an hedge of thorns...

This one really enters and brings problems. Every step this man takes is in bondage. How would you like your pathway to be nothing but a hedge of thorns?

The spirits of tiredness and laziness sometimes enter together. A person can yield to this lazy spirit so often that the spirit will take up his abode in the body. This person soon begins to wake up tired. He lives tired. As we confess, renounce and resist this spirit, it soon leaves. However, many times you may need outside help in getting deliverance.

One woman who had been continually tired, after being set free of this spirit, went home and worked all night cleaning her house.

Others have slept through church services until delivered from this.

Physical problems and/or overwork may exhaust our bodies. I do not refer to these; however, overwork can invite evil spirits also because resistance drops. Overwork is sin also because it is rebellion against God's natural laws for the body. You may think that you are being driven to overwork due to circumstances, but it is a sin against the body none the less.

SATAN ENTERS THROUGH CULTS

Deut. 18:10-11. There shall not be found among you anyone that maketh his son or daughter to pass through the fire, or that useth divination, or an observer of times, or an enchanter, or a witch, or a charmer, or a consulter with familiar spirits, or a wizard, or a necromancer.

Water witches; prediction by astrology; enchantments such as setting curses on others; witches; fortune tellers; a charmer such as one who puts you under hypnosis; a consulter with familiar spirits such as seances; mediums, levitation, ESP; and many other such like are demonic forces.

Anyone who has ever had any connection with these spirits should publicly renounce them and in many cases seek further help for deliverance.

Mic. 5:12. I will cut off witchcrafts out of thine hand; and thou shalt have no more soothsayers. Is. 47:9. But these two things shall come to thee in a moment in one day, the loss of children, and widowhood: they shall come upon thee in

their perfection for the multitude of thy sorceries, and for the great abundance of thine enchantments.

Is. 47:13. Thou art wearied in the multitude of thy counsels. Let now the astrologers, the stargazers, the monthly prognosticators, stand up, and save thee from these things that shall come upon thee. 14. Behold, they shall be as stubble; the fire shall burn them; they shall not deliver themselves from the power of the flame...

Rev. 18:23. And the light of the candle shall shine no more at all in thee; and the voice of the bridegroom and the bride shall be heard no more at all in thee: for the merchants were the great men of the earth; for by thy sorceries were all nations deceived.

"I will cut off witchcrafts out of thine hand." The Bible over and over brings condemnation upon witches because they are completely yielded over to Satan. They are Satan's representatives. He carries out much of his activity through those that will yield to him. Going to this type of individual to receive instructions will open your life to satanic power.

One lady was recently delivered from the curse of a witch (palm reader and/or fortune teller). She would constantly hear steps in her house. Satan would torment her at night with sleeplessness. He would make her feel like he was injecting needles into her body, causing her to madly claw at her body. After she was delivered from this curse she looked twenty years younger.

Is. 47:9 and 13 deal with astrologers, stargazers, monthly prognosticators, etc. Many are caught up with astrology and horoscope predictions. God says judgment will fall upon a nation that follows these spirits because she turns to evil spirits for a word rather than to the living God. Many folks get so "hooked" on this type of spirit that they are like an alcoholic; even when they find out that it is demon power, they don't want to give it up.

Rev. 18:23 speaks of judgment coming upon a people because they were caught up in sorceries. This word indicates in the Greek to enchant with drugs. This is the youth movement today. The Devil is the father of it. Unless it is corrected, it will bring complete downfall to our nation.

We could go on and on discussing the various cults such as ouija boards, ESP games, voodoo, Eastern religions, etc.

Speaking of ouija boards, I talked to a person who spoke day after day to the spirit that came to her while playing with the ouija board. It went with her for days until it entered her son. It would speak to her making wild suggestions such as: "Let's go get drunk. Let's go for a ride."

One lad defended the ouija board making a stand against "old fogie" ideas held by his mother. That night Satan visited him in his bedroom. He was glad to renounce it in the morning.

One lady, desiring to witness to her friends about the sin of the ouija board, went to her bedroom and bound the power that operated the ouija board in the name of Jesus Christ. The girls were heard to say, "What is wrong with it? It doesn't work any more." Then she made her witness to them for Jesus.

SATAN ENTERS THROUGH A REJECTED, SELF-PITY SPIRIT

Parents are admonished not to provoke their children to wrath. Eph. 6:4. Children through various reasons can develop a lonely, rejected, and timid spirit. This may be due to maladjustment to the parents. The parents arguing in front of the children can cause this easily. Over-correction of the children in a spirit of wrath can cause the child to rebel against the parent, or his reaction might be to feel lonely, sad, helpless, and unloved. As this attitude is nursed, it soon becomes a part of his or her life pattern. Children need correction, but it should be done in love and prayer.

One beautiful girl had such a bad spirit of rejection and self-pity that she would feel like crawling under a table when in the presence of others. Some of this spirit was ministered to her at home. Then it was fed by a teacher in the fifth grade. Every time the girl would make a slight mistake the teacher would say, "You are the most stupid girl that I have ever seen." This girl said that for years after this she would hear those words repeated over and over in her spirit. She was thoroughly convinced.

If she had been taught to rejoice in the Lord regardless, then nothing could have touched her. But on the contrary, she yielded to this idea. It became an active seed growing stronger and stronger in her being. I am glad to report that she was delivered in Jesus' name.

Parents need to teach their children joy. Live a life of victory and joy before your children. Phil. 4:4 says, "Rejoice in the Lord alway." Regardless of the problem, learn to rejoice. Teach the child to respond with victory regardless of the situation. Constantly yielding over to spirits of sadness, fear, failure, frustration, and such like bring Satan into your life. You then will have problems of nervousness, uncertainty, timidity, and with these may come sickness. These will remain the rest of your life unless exposed, dealt with, and cast out.

Adults can pick these up through being beaten down by the opposite sex, especially in the case of a wife being overridden by a dominating spirit in the husband. Her only hope is to rejoice regardless. If she begins to defend herself, she probably will pick up a harsh, fighting, critical, mean spirit. As she yields over to a confused, frustrated, self-pity spirit she begins to withdraw into her little shell (dream world).

Men may pick up a timid self-pity spirit due to problems in childhood. They may have been overridden by a domineering mother. This could have taught them early to submit to that spirit. Then they pick a refuge in this type of personality for a wife. Also, there are times when a woman ends up with this type of husband; she finds it almost a necessity to move into a dominant role to keep things moving. (Perhaps she had a domineering mother who passed this spirit on to her. Then she just keeps expecting this spirit in her husband to yield to her just as her father yielded to her mother. This tends to keep the poor man bound in chains of timidity and rejection.) Jesus can help in any situation.

Sometimes children feel frustrated competing with different abilities in older or younger children in the family. To take up their slack in achievements they will rebel and do anything to make trouble just to get recognition.

Parents need to counsel their children to be individuals in their own right to prevent this from happening.

One lady picked up an inferiority or timid, self-pity,spirit as a child through a conflict with her mother. After she forgave her mother, the spirit left. While I was casting the spirit out, it began to scream in a harsh voice: "God does not love this woman. God does not love this woman." After it left, she cried out in heavenly devotion and love, "He loves me, He loves me." Satan had convinced her that no one loved her, not even God.

SATAN ENTERS THROUGH THE ABUSE OF THE TONGUE

Pr. 12:18...The tongue of the wise is health.
Pr. 13:3. He that keepeth his mouth keepeth his life: but he that openeth wide his lips shall have destruction.
Pr. 12:13. The wicked is snared by the transgression of the lips: but the just shall come out of trouble.

"The tongue of the wise is health." Words of faith produce victory. Speak words of healing such as "By His stripes I am healed," or "He healeth all of my diseases." One man confessed words of faith over his daughter morning and night until a spastic child was completely healed.

God's nature is built into us through His Word. 2 Pet. 1:4. "Whereby are given unto us exceeding great and precious promises: that by these (promises) ye might be partakers of the divine nature." Jn. 14:23 teaches us that Jesus will come and take up His abode in us as we keep His Word. His Word will heal. His Word will give growth. His Word will bring you to new heights.

Speaking negative words of criticism, failure, nobody loves me, hate, poverty, weakness, allows Satan, the father of these spirits, to enter. Whoever you yield yourselves to, his servant you become. "He that openeth his mouth wide shall have destruction." Your lips release a flow from the heart. As you yield to God, He flows through your heart and lips and creates victory. As you yield to Satan, he flows through your heart and lips and creates his nature, defeat.

So Pr. 12:13 says we are snared, or we come out of trouble, by our lips.

One reaps what he sows. Read Gal. 6:7-8: "Be not deceived; God is not mocked: for whatsoever a man soweth, that shall he also reap. For he that soweth to the flesh shall of the flesh reap corruption; but he that soweth to the Spirit shall of the Spirit reap life everlasting."

Words and thoughts are spirits. They are

either from God or the enemy. Yield to positive truths from God's Word, and they will build the very life of God in you. Yield to thoughts or words of negative nature, and they will produce the defeat of Satan in you. Whichever spirit you yield to will soon dominate you. Every negative thought and word you speak or think soon builds up that idea and nature in you. Go to the word and let it build the very nature of God into you. God enters through His Word. Jn. 14:23. **Pr. 15:4. A wholesome tongue is a tree of life: but perverseness therein is a breach in the spirit.**

Once when I was around much sickness, I felt immune to it. I was sailing above it. I had no sense of warfare with it. However, I began to speak negatively concerning a sinner in the church. Immediately I felt a breach in my spirit. I felt an instant attack from Satan. My negative confession and conversation opened my life to demonic forces. I instantly repented and confessed this. God removed it. I felt the infirm spirit lift.

I saw another brother get an extreme case of flu right in the midst of a great deliverance campaign. God spoke to him and told him that this was an attack of Satan which was allowed to enter through his critical spirit toward a fellow minister.

SATAN ENTERS THROUGH ABNORMAL GRIEF

Pr. 17:22. A merry heart doeth good like a medicine: but a broken spirit drieth the bones.

Ps. 30:5...Weeping may endure for a night, but joy cometh in the morning.

A merry heart is like a medicine. A broken spirit drieth the bones and bringeth sickness. Weeping may come, but make sure you get your joy back instantly. Is. 12:3, "Therefore with joy shall ye draw water out of the wells of salvation." Learn to draw on God's power by yielding to joy spirits rather than sad spirits. Joy brings God into your life. Sadness brings Satan. Make up your mind which you prefer.

Many elderly people yield to a sad, lonely spirit due to the departure of a loved one. This soon brings them into much bondage; more sadness; and with this, sickness. We have seen many set free from this spirit in Jesus' name.

In times of great disaster folks are prone to yield to shock and fear, etc. One person came to me with everything wrong with her. I found ut that the sickness began to develop about the time her son, daughter-in-law, and three grandchildren had been killed in a car accident.

Just to mention it caused her to go into hysterics, even though the accident had occurred six years previously.

Train yourself to stay above your problems rather than to get down under them.

SATAN ENTERS THROUGH FEAR

1 Jn. 4:18. There is no fear in love; but perfect love casteth out fear: because fear hath torment.

Torment is a devil. Fear so controls some that they are afraid to enter a house alone. Others

23

fear to drive or ride in a car after having an accident. There are many types of fear. The scriptures say that God did not give the spirit of fear. 2 Tim. 1:7. So we know it is of the devil.

Ps. 27:1, "The Lord is my light and my salvation; whom shall I fear?" This is God's way. Declare boldly that God is your deliverance and refuse to become a slave to Satan.

Ps. 23:4, "Yea, though I walk through the valley of the shadow of death, I will fear no evil." Train yourself to yield to joy and strength and peace rather than fear and death.

Gen. 15:1, "...Fear not, Abram: I am thy shield, and thy exceeding great reward." Fear opens the door to the enemy. One missionary was sick unto death. The Lord spoke to him and said, "If you will not let fear enter, I will heal you."

The earthly response to problems and sickness is to yield to fear. This stops the perfect flow of faith. God moves in peace, joy, gentleness and victory. Train yourself to respond to every situation with joy and peace. This releases the faith flow from heaven.

SATAN ENTERS THROUGH DENOMINATIONAL DOGMAS

The Lord has told us to have no other gods before us. Yet many are so bound by denominational spirits that they twist the scriptures to make them fit their "line." One group of deacons said, "We don't care what the Word of God says, this is not our church doctrine."

I used to twist the scripture to fit my denominational approach. Now I let the scripture shave and cut on me.

SATAN ENTERS THROUGH HATE

Mt. 5:39...Resist not evil: but whosoever shall smite thee on thy right cheek, turn to him the other also. 44. Love your enemies...
Rom. 12:17. Recompense no man evil for evil...
1 Jn. 2:9. He that saith he is in the light, and hateth his brother, is in darkness...

One woman so hated her father for having abused her sexually that an extremely critical and frustrated spirit dominated her. Everyone else was wrong in her thinking. She was so possessed with evil spirits that once they were stirred up, it was impossible to talk to or contact the natural human spirit. The evil spirit would answer back instead.

Another man was so filled with hate for a church that had condemned him and his girlfriend, that Satan completely possessed his body. Upon rebuking the Devil, the man would be completely dominated with Satanic words and actions. Satan would make him twist like a snake. He would throw him to the ground. We could not get the demon out until this hate and bitterness were removed through repentance.

Chapter 4

THE RESULTS OF SATAN'S ENTRANCE
INTO THE INDIVIDUAL

WHEN SATAN ENTERS HE BRINGS SICKNESS, WEAKNESS, FRUSTRATION AND FEAR

Ps. 34:12-14. What man is he that desireth life, and loveth many days, that he may see good? Keep thy tongue from evil, and thy lips from speaking guile. Depart from evil, and do good; seek peace, and pursue it.

Yielding to evil and criticism shortens your life. It is like drinking poison.

Ps. 31:10. For my life is spent with grief, and my years with sighing: my strength faileth because of mine iniquity, and my bones are consumed.

Sorrow, sadness, and sickness are all attributed to yielding to these Satanic attitudes.

Acts 10:38. How God anointed Jesus of Nazareth with the Holy Ghost and with power: who went about doing good, and healing all that were oppressed of the devil; for God was with him.

God calls sickness an oppression of the devil.

Job 2:7. So went Satan forth from the presence of the Lord, and smote Job with sore boils.

In this case Satan brought boils. Job's own testimony was, "The thing I greatly feared came upon me." Perhaps this opened the door to all of his sickness.

Mt. 4:24...They brought unto him all sick people that were taken with divers diseases and torments, and those which were possessed with devils, and those which were lunatic, and those that had the palsy; and He healed them.

All of these people were called sick people. The scripture does explain the different types of sickness such as torments, complete demon possession, lunatics, palsy, etc.

Not all sickness is direct demonic activity; however, you can be sure that he has had something to do with it directly or indirectly.

Nervous breakdowns come from demonic forces working in the individual life. We have seen cases of frustration, fear, and uncertainty which would point to a direct act of Satan.

We have had cases of girls who had been molested by close relatives. In the cases that we have dealt with, confusion, frustration, nervousness, and many other conditions followed. In some cases shock was followed by a complete nervous breakdown. In other cases a complete sex block was set up. One girl actually feared for a man to touch her arm. When this girl was delivered she was set free from all of this fear of man.

Harmony in the home is disrupted by demonic forces working in one or more in that family.

Abnormal response to authority and law is demonic activity. One lad asked me to cast out the spirit of disrespect for law and order. Immediately upon rebuking this, the devil said through the lad, "Stop pushing me around.

Nobody is going to push me around." He came out in Jesus' name.

Many cases of sex perversion are a result of frustrations in childhood. One girl was mistreated by the family. She was made to work as a man but treated as a slave. She hated the day she was born a girl. This hatred grew. She hated her lot in life. She hated her father and brothers. Soon her entire sex drive was changed to that of a man. She became a lesbian. She was delivered of this as she confessed her problem and repented.

In many cases of alcoholism we have found the problem stemmed from childhood. As adulthood developed, the problems of youth were converted to adult problems and the turmoil increased.

Some seek to find refuge in extreme criticism and hate. Others have turned to alcohol to try to forget it all. Whether it be worry, hate, frustration, or alcohol, it is still a demon spirit in which one has sought refuge rather than God.

Chapter 5

HOW TO GET DELIVERANCE FROM
DEMONIC FORCES

It is very important to find the root problem. Go back to when you first noticed your symptoms. It may go back to childhood. Perhaps fear of man or insecurity, due to childhood turmoil, has caused the problems. Perhaps rebellion to parental authority during your teen-age years brought much Satanic activity into your life.

Pray and ask the Lord to reveal this to you. Go back through your life and check out the rough spots. At each problem point in your life ask the Lord to forgive the person or persons involved regardless of the situation; ask the Lord to forgive you for your negative reaction to that situation. (Even though in many cases you did it in ignorance.) Ask the Lord to heal this section of your life and attitude. It may be that you will have to do this several times before you get release.

Remember, in all of these suggestions on deliverance that these are general to cover many situations. You may get delivered by obedience to any one of these suggestions. God is God. He will deliver when your heart reaches Him. We don't get delivered by a set of rules; however, these things listed here are scriptural, and they will help you to find your way through the "fog" to complete deliverance.

We have not dealt with the gift of miracles in this book. The miracle power of God is far beyond our wildest expectation. God can break through to you; and when He does, Satan leaves with no argument.

Primarily, however, we have not dealt with the gift of miracles, or even the word of knowledge (which shows our root problem), but we have dealt with your faith just as you are right now.

WE MUST FORSAKE SIN

Jn. 5:14...Sin no more, lest a worse thing come unto thee.

Jesus had healed this man who had been a cripple; then he admonished him to cease from sinning or a worse thing would come. I have seen dope addicts delivered and walk in victory for days; then, due to a spirit of anger or hate, the spirits of dope were allowed to return.

One alcoholic was set free in Jesus' name; after one year he decided to prove that he had power in himself to control it. He started drinking just to prove that he could handle it. Now he is worse than he was before.

One Christian insisted on fellowshipping another person who believed in spiritualism, etc. This Christian became so controlled by evil spirits that they would come back as fast as they were driven out. Later, when this Christian renounced all relationships with this other individual, complete deliverance came.

WE MUST WALK IN LOVE

2 Cor. 5:14. For the love of Christ constraineth us...
Col. 3:14. Above all these things put on love, which is the bond of perfectness.
Pr. 10:12. Hatred stirreth up strifes; but love covereth all sins.
Gal. 5:6...Faith which worketh by love.

God is love. As we walk in love, we walk in the very presence of God. Walking in hate, revenge, or critical, negative spirits is walking in Satanic influence. Love will bring you into perfection, or maturity, and completeness. Hatred makes you meaner because you are yielding over to Satan, but love exalts Christ and makes you more like Him. The more you yield to love, the more deliverance you will receive.

Learn to love that husband who is mistreating you. Learn to love those with whom you work. Love as Christ loved. Jn. 15:9.

In Mt. 5:44 Jesus said, "Love your enemies, bless them that curse you, do good to them that hate you, and pray for them which despitefully use you, and persecute you."

Often we justify ourselves because others mistreat us. Regardless of your problem or situation, it is absolutely essential that you yield to love.. Turn on the joy "button". "Rejoice in the Lord always, and again I say rejoice." Phil. 4:4. Away with that negative "poor little ole me" spirit. You are God's favorite child. You are the apple of His eye. Turn on the love of Jesus for others, and don't forget to love yourself, also. Satan will accuse you. If you have sinned, confess it. Refuse to let the accuser work on you any longer.

RIGHT ATTITUDE

Pr. 23:7. As he thinketh in his heart, so is he.
Jer. 6:19...I will bring evil upon this people, even the fruit of their thoughts...
Ps. 37:4. Delight thyself also in the Lord; and he shall give thee the desires of thine heart.
Pr. 21:5. The thoughts of the diligent tend only to plenteousness; but of every one that is hasty only to want.

Whatever you think, you become. Negative thoughts bring judgment, problems, and failure. Setting your heart on Jesus brings victory. Your thoughts actually create victories as you move in the Holy Spirit. Actions of negative nature and failure are yielding to Satan. They cause you to be in bondage to Satan.

Keep the victory flowing through you regardless of your situation. Learn to praise God whether you feel like it or not.

Complaining, griping, and talking about your problems merely create a fertile field for the Devil to work in your life.

FAST AND PRAY

Is. 58:8. Then shall thy light break forth as the morning, and thine health shall spring forth speedily: and thy righteousness shall go before thee; the glory of the Lord shall be thy reward.

Here God revealed the fast was to be more

than just going without food. It must be accompanied with genuine repentance and change of heart. All stingy spirits must leave. There must be a completely new outlook upon life. Then health will flow. A negative outlook to everything will soon create many problems in many areas of your life.

Fasting causes the body to come into line with the will of the Spirit. It subdues the normal fleshly activities. Paul declares, "I keep under my body, and bring it into subjection." 1 Cor. 9:27.

Satan attacks the body many times to gain a foothold into one's life. Read the struggle in Rom. 7:22-23: "I delight in the law of God after the inward man: But I see another law in my members, warring against the law of my mind, and bringing me into captivity..."

2 Cor. 11:27...In fasting often.

It is necessary to get serious with God. It won't take long to overcome most of the problems if a person goes on several ten-day complete fasts (water only).

Fasting is only one way God has for deliverance. Many folks have been set free of serious conditions without fasting.

A life moving on with God will be one that fasts often. Especially is this true for our leaders who are called to pave the way for others. Many victories come by "fastings often."

Phil. 3:19. Whose end is destruction, whose God is their belly...

Much sickness can be traced back to overeating. A fast will help cure this.

Another form of discipline would be a partial

33

fast. Put yourself on a juice breakfast and lunch with only one full meal and no in-between lunches or samples. Daniel had a similar time which he called "mourning." Dan. 10:2. During this time he cut back on some of his luxury type eating. Dan. 10:3. Do not confuse this with a full fast. Dan 9:3 speaks of the complete fast.

2 Chr. 33:12. When he was in affliction, he besought the Lord his God, and humbled himself greatly before the God of his fathers.

Through this prayer and fasting God delivered Manasseh. Whether your affliction is an enemy trying to destroy you or a disease, it is still from Satan. God is no respecter of persons; He will deliver you, also.

Many reports have come from people who have been delivered of cancer and tumors, gray hair has turned to black, youthful attitudes have been renewed, etc., through fasting. In some cases it is the longer fasts of forty days or more, with water only, that bring deliverance.

HUNGER AFTER GOD

Ps. 107:9. He satisfieth the longing soul, and filleth the hungry soul with goodness.
Is. 44:3. I will pour water upon him that is thirsty, and floods upon the dry ground: I will pour my spirit upon thy seed, and my blessing upon thine offspring.
Pr. 2:4-5. If thou seekest her as silver, and searchest for her as for hid treasures; then shalt thou understand the fear of the Lord, and find the knowledge of God.

Get serious with God. He satisfieth the

longing soul. He filleth the hungry soul with goodness. He pours water upon him that is thirsty. He pours floods upon dry ground. As we seek after Him as for hid treasures, then we understand God. Then we find God in a new dimension. Then we get deliverance. Many need deliverance from unbelief. This attitude of unbelief that rests upon the body of Christ can be lifted by hungering after God. When this happens, nothing shall be impossible with the true believer. Mt. 17:20.

Many folks are healed without getting serious with God, but too often the enemy is back before they get home from church or shortly thereafter. Yielding to our old way of life will draw demon forces right back to us. They will return by the same route that they entered the first time.

GET HUMBLE BEFORE GOD

Mt. 23:12...He that shall humble himself shall be exalted.
James 4:6...God resisteth the proud, but giveth grace unto the humble.
Mt. 5:6. Blessed are they which do hunger and thirst after righteousness: for they shall be filled.
2 Chr. 7:14. If my people, which are called by my name, shall humble themselves, and pray, and seek my face, and turn from their wicked ways; then will I hear from heaven, and will forgive their sin, and will heal their land.

As you humble yourself before God and seek His face, He gives you a lift. On the other hand,

God will be repelled and turn from the proud spirit because it is a demonic spirit. So God promises deliverance for the spirit that comes before Him in honesty and complete surrender.

YOU MUST HAVE A FORGIVING SPIRIT

Mt. 18:34-35. And his lord was wroth, and delivered him to the tormentors, till he should pay all that was due unto him. So likewise shall my heavenly Father do also unto you, if ye from your hearts forgive not every one his brother their trespasses.

This man refused to forgive his fellow man a trivial sum of money when he himself had been forgiven a large, large debt. For this ungrateful and ungodly act of unforgiveness the man was thrown to the tormentors.

Jesus has forgiven us an infinite debt of sin. If we refuse to forgive our fellow man some trivial sin, then God will be forced to turn us over to the tormentor. "So likewise shall my heavenly Father do also unto you, if you from your hearts forgive not every one his brother his trespasses." One person had a great problem for which she could not find healing and deliverance. The Spirit of God showed me that she hated and would not forgive her mother. I spoke to her about this. Instantly she screamed out, "I hate my mother! I hate my mother!" Needless to say, she did not get deliverance.

One teenage girl so hated and would not forgive her dad that Satan would return as fast as I could cast him out. Later this same girl did repent and received deliverance.

I have seen others, upon repentance and forgiveness of those against whom they had held long-standing grudges, instantly and gloriously delivered.

This is true of those who are angry with God. Repent. Ask the Lord to forgive you. In cases where you blame God, your problem is not God at all. It is Satan taking advantage of situations, attitudes, and weaknesses. You are never right to blame God. He never makes a mistake. Any "God blaming" spirit that you might have is certainly the devil.

Mk. 11:25. When ye stand praying, forgive, if ye have ought against any: that your Father also which is in heaven may forgive you your trespasses.

There is no short cut. It is mandatory to forgive and forsake all grudges.

WE MUST CONFESS SIN

James 5:16. Confess your faults one to another, and pray one for another, that ye may be healed.

1 Jn. 1:9. If we confess our sins, he is faithful and just to forgive us our sins, and to cleanse us from all unrighteousness.

This is God's plan. Confess it out. Expose it. Renounce it. Forsake it. Deliverance will follow.

Many times I have struggled with men who have had demon spirits. As soon as they would confess their guilt, the evil spirit would leave. I have seen other men confess their sin and have no visible signs of deliverance at that moment, yet from that time on they were delivered. One man confessed that he had a terrible lust problem. I suggested that he confide in his wife, and the two of them then pray about it. He needed no further deliverance.   Satan cannot stand to be exposed. He hates the light and the truth. You cannot hide behind your sin and expect to get deliverance.

YOU MUST HAVE A TENDER SPIRIT

Is. 53:2. For he shall grow up before him as a tender plant...
Mt. 5:39...Resist not evil: but whosoever shall smite thee on they right cheek, turn to him the other also.
2 Tim. 2:24. The servant of the Lord must not strive; but be gentle unto all men...
James 3:17. The wisdom that is from above is first pure, then peaceable, gentle, and easy to be entreated, full of mercy and good fruits...

A rough, harsh spirit is Satanic. This spirit draws evil spirits into one's life. Forsake this harsh, mean way and attitude of life.

"Resist not evil." Don't stand up for your rights. Be tender. Be kind. Be loving. Turn the other cheek. Jesus will work it out. A fighting spirit only draws more evil spirits into your life and makes the situation worse. A tender, trusting spirit turns the situation over to Jesus. Let the Lord do your fighting back. Let the Lord be your defense. You will have fewer battles. Stand still and see the salvation of the Lord.

"The servant of the Lord must not strive." A

constant warfare going on within your own spirit or that of your family merely sows a seed for demonic activity. The fruit of the spirit is love, joy, and peace. Regardless of your circumstances, you should never manifest a Satanic, striving spirit. Some women develop a terrible striving spirit because they have a very mean and domineering husband. Develop the joy spirit regardless of your situation. Now you are on the road to a permanent deliverance.

Jesus moved in a tender, loving, compassionate spirit. This is the Holy Spirit's way for you. Don't get Jesus' manifestations of anger confused with fleshly anger. At times the Spirit would move upon Him, and He would say and do hard things. (Such as driving the animals from the temple and overturning the money changers' tables.)

"The wisdom that is from above is first pure, then peaceable, gentle, and easy to be entreated..." Are you forever telling people off, or are you gentle and easy to be entreated?

Mt. 11:29, "Take my yoke upon you, and learn of me; for I am meek and lowly in heart: and ye shall find rest unto your souls." The tender, restful spirit is the Jesus spirit. This will bring healing to your spirit and body.

FILL YOURSELF WITH THE WORD OF GOD

Lk. 11:24. When the unclean spirit is gone out of a man, he walketh through dry places, seeking rest; and finding none, he saith, I will return unto my house whence I came out. 25. And when he cometh, he findeth it swept and

39

garnished. **26. Then goeth he, and taketh to him seven other spirits more wicked than himself; and they enter in, and dwell there: and the last state of the man is worse than the first.**

Let God's Word find its place in your life. Walk in the Word. The Word builds Christ into your life. Jn. 14:23, "...If a man love me, he will keep my words: and my Father will love him, and we will come unto him, and make our abode with him."

As your life is filled with the Word of God, then it is filled with the Father and the Son. This builds strength and resistance to Satan.

If your life is not filled with the Word and things of the Spirit, then it can be invaded by Satan. You are either going to have God in your thoughts or negative forces. Train yourself to move and think according to the victorious Word of God.

AVAIL YOURSELF OF THE BLOOD OF JESUS CHRIST

Rev. 12:11. And they overcame him by the blood of the Lamb, and by the word of their testimony; and they loved not their lives unto the death.
1 Jn. 1:9. If we confess our sins, he is faithful and just to forgive us our sins, and to cleanse us from all unrighteousness.
1 Jn. 1:7. But if we walk in the light, as he is in the light, we have fellowship one with another, and the blood of Jesus Christ His Son cleanseth us from all sin.

Satan hates the blood of Jesus. While casting a

demon out of a lad one day, we began to sing about the blood of Jesus. The demon began to scream out, "Leave the blood out, leave the blood out." He could not stand the blood. The lad was instantly delivered.

Satan hates light and purity in our life. As we walk in the light of the Lord then we are cleansed from all sin by the blood of Jesus. Come to Jesus. Repent. Then stand tall in your pardon and forgiveness. Don't let self-condemnation come upon you. Just keep shouting the victory. Do not allow yourself to be brought back into a guilt complex. He has forgiven you. He has removed your sin. Now refuse to listen to the accuser any longer.

They overcame the Devil by their testimony and by the blood. They confessed that in Jesus they were more than conquerors. They confessed that through the blood of Jesus they were no longer guilty. It was as though they had never sinned.

DEVELOP A WORSHIP AND VICTORY SPIRIT

Ep. 5:19. Speaking to yourselves in psalms and hymns and spiritual songs, singing and making melody in your heart to the Lord.
Judges 5:3...I will sing unto the Lord...
Learn to sing the Word of God by the hour. Keep a sweet melody flowing out of your spirit. This keeps your soul clean and fresh. Make your own melody. You may sound flat and feel awkward at first. Once you develop your melody, then it will flow and flow. You can take one verse and sing it over and over applying it

41

to your needs, as well as those of others, as you go about your daily activities. Practice abiding in the Word of God.

Ps. 34:1. I will bless the Lord at all times: His praise shall continually be in my mouth.

Pr. 27:21. As the fining pot for silver, and the furnace for gold; so is a man to his praise.

Ps. 74:21. Let not the oppressed return ashamed: let the poor and needy praise thy name.

Ps. 22:3. Thou art holy, O thou that inhabitest the praises of Israel.

Ps. 67:5-6. Let the people praise thee, O God; let all the people praise thee. Then shall the earth yield her increase; and God, even our own God, shall bless us.

Let the victory praise to Jesus be continually in your mouth rather than a negative report.

Praise will purge and purify just as the furnace will purify the gold.

The oppressed does not return ashamed because he praises the name of the Lord and is thereby set free.

As the saints learn to praise God, they shall see an increase in deliverance and power. So let there be a constant flow of victory and worship out of your heart to the Heavenly Father. "God abides in the midst of the praise of His people." As you yield to joy and worship and praise, you draw God into your life. As you yield to complaining and such like, you draw Satanic forces into your life.

IN ALL THINGS GIVE THANKS

Ps. 31:24. Be of good courage, and he shall

strengthen your heart...

Pr. 17:22. A merry heart doeth good like a medicine: but a broken spirit drieth the bones.

Neh. 8:10...Neither be ye sorry; for the joy of the Lord is your strength.

Is. 12:3. With joy shall ye draw water out of the wells of salvation.

Phil. 4:4. Rejoice in the Lord alway...

1 Thes. 5:18. In everything give thanks: for this is the will of God in Christ Jesus concerning you.

Eph. 5:20. Giving thanks always for all things unto God... in the name of our Lord Jesus Christ.

"Be of good courage, and he shall strengthen thine heart." This is God's way. Take a positive step of faith. Be of good courage by faith; then the victory and strength follow.

"Neither be ye sorry; for the joy of the Lord is your strength." Yielding to sadness brings bondage. Yielding to joy and victory brings deliverance. Work much on the victory spirit. Have a victorious outlook at all times regardless of outward appearances. This might be difficult at times, but it can be developed.

Notice that it is with joy that we draw water out of the wells of salvation. Joy usually accompanies deliverance. I have seen folks begin to praise and shout unto the Lord and deliverance came.

"In everthing give thanks." "Giving thanks always for all things." This is the will of God in Christ Jesus for you. Everything works out for good to those who love the Lord. Treat every test as an exam for promotion. Rejoice your way through. Regardless of your problem, shout and praise the Lord. Your burden will go quickly. Your sickness will soon vanish.

As we thank the Lord for everthing, we are saying, "Hallelujah, here is another opportunity for the Lord to shew himself strong on my behalf." Make yourself have a "ball" everytime you have a problem. Rejoice and laugh and praise God at the least sign of trouble or sickness. This will create such relaxation and peace that it will release your faith flow. The Lord will flow out through this peace and joy and set the captive free.

Sickness and problems multiply in the atmosphere of fear, sadness, worry, etc. Meet each problem, regardless of its size, with joy, rejoicing and thanksgiving. Fear will lift. Satan will have a nervous breakdown and flee. Deliverance is thine.

OUR BODY IS A TEMPLE FOR THE HOLY GHOST

Eph. 2:22. In whom ye also are builded together for an habitation of God through the Spirit. 1 Cor. 6:19. What? Know ye not that your body is the temple of the Holy Ghost which is in you, which ye have of God, and ye are not your own? 20. Ye are bought with a price: therefore glorify God in your body, and in your spirit, which are God's.

Legally you belong to Jesus. Illegally you have yielded certain areas of your life to Satan. Through this illegal yielding of the will to Satan he has somewhat of a legal entrance into your life.

Generally speaking, Satan enters through the mind. Much of his work is carried out in the fleshly body. Along with this, he oppresses the spirit. In the case of one completely yielded to him, he possesses the spirit.

Renounce any hold that Satan may have on you. Confess your sin. Repent. Break this hold he has in your life. Confess it now that your body belongs to the Lord and not to demon powers. Refuse to stay in bondage to him any longer.

Just as the wife belongs to her husband and not to other men, so you belong to Jesus, and not to oppressing spirits, if you are a child of God. Put your foot down against these intruding forces. They have no more right there than strange men have a right in the life of a man's wife.

A Christian is violating his spiritual marriage vows by yielding to demonic forces. Repent of this. There is forgiveness through the blood of Jesus. Return to your first love in all operations of your life. Renounce these evil intruders once and for all. Call them for what they are. They are "hoodlum" spirits. They have no part in your life. "Boot" them out of your life now!

The non-Christian is delivered basically the same as the Christian. He comes in Jesus' name asking forgiveness for his sins. Sinners in Jesus' day merely said, "Lord, help."

THE WORD FOR SPIRIT IN THE GREEK MEANS BREATH AND/OR AIR

Jn. 20:22 **And when he had said this, he**

breathed on them, and saith unto them, Receive ye the Holy Ghost.

There was no sin in Jesus. He was pure and holy. When He, by faith, breathed on them, the Holy Ghost flowed through His breath.

Mt. 8:16...They brought unto him many that were possessed with devils: and he cast out the spirits with his word...

The Greek word here for spirit means air. Evil spirits as well as the Holy Spirit have a relationship with air and breathing. When the Lord made man, He breathed into his nostrils the breath of life. The same Hebrew word used for breath here was later used for spirit in Job and Proverbs.

We have seen many manisfestations in the area of the breath in casting out devils. Some scream; others cry with loud voices; others moan, foam at the mouth, cough, yawn, burp, etc. You can find similar manifestations in the New Testament.

Some time ago I laid my hands on a lad in Jesus' name and merely said, "Lord Jesus, set him free." Instantly he exhaled violently three times. He was instantly delivered and began to shout and praise God.

This has happened several times during other deliverance sessions. Many times I will encourage a person to take a deep breath and exhale by faith in Jesus' name. This has released the faith of the individual and deliverance has come.

If you repent and seek the Lord, you can do this yourself. Many get their own deliverance at home. You may feel a lump or pressure coming up from within your chest or abdomen. Continue to exhale slowly but forcefully (too fast may make you dizzy). This pressure may come right on up, hit your throat, and cause you to want to cough. You might gag a little with it. Each case is different. Force this out by coughing, etc., if necessary. With this may come phlegm or foam depending on the type of spirit, even varying in color and contents.

Some deliverances are very dramatic. The devil may scream, cry, or throw the person around while being cast out. Other spirits pass out through other parts of the body such as the head or hands. Others just disappear with no manifestations.

Chapter 6

ALL BELIEVERS HAVE
AUTHORITY OVER DEMONS

Lk. 9:1. Then he called his twelve disciples together, and gave them power and authority over all devils, and to cure diseases.
Lk. 10:19. I give unto you power to tread on serpents and scorpions, and over all the power of the enemy: and nothing shall by any means hurt you.
Mk. 16:17. These signs shall follow them that believe; In my name shall they cast out devils...
Jn. 14:12..He that believeth on me, the works that I do shall he do also; and greater works than these shall he do; because I go unto my Father.

Upon studying these scriptures you will see that He first gave the power to the apostles. Then in Lk. 10:19 He gave this power to the seventy lay preachers. Then in Mk. 16:17 He declared that this power and authority was for every believer in Christ.

Christ is in the believer. Satan is afraid of Christ. "You resist the devil, and he will flee from you." James 4:7. However, just before this the scripture declares, "Submit yourselves therefore to God." Then in the following verse, James 4:8, "Draw nigh to God, and he will draw nigh to you. Cleanse your hands, ye sinners; and purify your hearts, ye double minded." In

48

all of this we are exhorting you to walk with the Lord and recognize that you have authority over devils in Jesus' name.

We use the believers in ministering deliverance. The job is too great and the time is too short for one man to take upon himself this tremendous task of bringing deliverance to the multitudes that seek help. God often uses the individual believer in the revelation ministry while ministering deliverance. The body of Christ is an important factor in deliverance. Many times we will start the demon spirit moving out and then ask one or two believers to take over and continue the deliverance; I then move on to another need. We need to learn to work together. We need to move into our ministry, also. Never be afraid of the Devil. He is afraid of you.

The only time that Satan could enter a person during a deliverance session is for that person to furnish him a fertile ground. We have seen folks resent a deliverance minister or the deliverance itself, and then later end up with the same symptoms present in the person being delivered. Rebellion, sin, and many other problems that violate the truths of the word of God can allow you to pick up evil spirits. (Even more so during a deliverance service.) So keep the right attitude within, and you will be secure.

CAN A BELIEVER TAKE AUTHORITY OVER EVIL SPIRITS IN OTHERS NOT PRESENT?

Jesus did in Mt. 15:22-28 when He cast the

tormenting spirit out of the woman's daughter. Jesus did it in Mt. 8:13 when He healed the centurion's servant. Other cases are recorded in the Bible of Jesus doing similar things.

This is in essence what God did through Paul in Acts 19:12, "So that from his body were brought unto the sick handkerchiefs or aprons, and the diseases departed from them, and the evil spirits went out of them."

Kenneth Hagin did this in Denver, Colo. He cast the spirit out of a girl who was then in a hospital in California. She was instantly delivered.

We have seen this in our ministry when we have demanded the infirm spirit to leave others as we joined in prayer, and the person, not present, was delivered in that very hour.

One lady in our services just recently moved in the spirit and commanded a man to leave a bar. Within fifteen minutes the man walked into the church and was saved.

In Mt. 18:18 the Lord tells us, "Whatsoever ye shall bind on earth shall be bound in heaven." So it is up to us to do the binding. However, this must be in the Spirit. We are not dictators over another person's will. God knows the heart and can bring deliverance. We must learn to flow softly in the will of God. So stir thyself up. Get up from the sidelines of do nothing. Dare to step out into the flow of the Spirit. You will soon find your place with the Lord.

The basis of the believer's authority is the name of Jesus Christ.

Chapter 7

MANIFESTATION OF DEMONS

SEDUCING SPIRITS

1 Tim. 4:1...In the latter times some shall depart from the faith, giving heed to seducing spirits and doctrines of devils.

It will be, and is, the characteristic of the end time to find spirits drawing true believers away from the truth either by outright demon manifestations or by subtle and seducing manners. Notice that this spirit works by getting believers to depart from the faith. To do so, he generally has to work cunningly so the individual will not be aware of his activities. Be cautious of spirits that keep telling you that his truth can only be seen by special revelation, etc. Be cautious of spirits that will ignore the general teaching of certain truths and teach opposites.

COMPLETE DEMON POSSESSION

Mt. 8:28-29...There met him two possessed with devils, coming out of tombs, exceeding fierce, so that no man might pass by that way...they cried out, saying, what have we to do with thee, Jesus, thou Son of God? Art thou come hither to torment us before the time?

This is complete demon possession. Satan controlled every part of this man. Satan will take all you give him. Don't let him have any part of you; he will only demand more and more.

BLIND AND DUMB SPIRITS

Mt. 12:22...One possessed with a devil, blind, and dumb.

Notice here the Lord calls just partial possession a demon possession. He was only possessed in the eyes and speech. The Bible is not dogmatic about this. Possession could refer to complete possession or only partial.

There are many Christians and non-Christians who have spirits of blindness or are deaf mutes.

This is not suggesting that every case of blindness or dumbness is an evil spirit. Directly or indirectly he was the cause of it. Had there been no devil, there would have been no problem. Heaven certainly will not have blindness, etc.

I have seen more blind eyes opened by casting out the devil of blindness than just praying. Let it be understood; one operating in miracle faith need only say, "Be healed in Jesus' name," and spirits of all nature leave. There is no set pattern with the Holy Ghost in ministering deliverance.

TORMENTING SPIRITS

Mt. 15:22...My daughter is grievously vexed with a devil.

Spirits tormented this girl day and night. She had no rest. Her life was a constant turmoil. She was filled with confusion. She had no peace.

Jesus cast this one out by proxy. He prayed for her at the request of the mother. Jesus set the captive free.

UNCLEAN SPIRITS

Lk. 9:39. Lo, a spirit taketh him, and he suddenly crieth out; and it teareth him that he foameth again, and bruising him hardly departeth from him. 42. And as he was yet a coming, the devil threw him down, and tare him. And Jesus rebuked the unclean spirit, and healed the child, and delivered him again to his father. delivered him again to his father.
Mk. 1:26. And when the unclean spirit had torn him, and cried with a loud voice, he came out of him.

It is nothing uncommon to hear spirits scream and cry out as they come out of people. At times people feel like the inside of their throat or other areas of their body have been torn. This sensation usually lasts only a few hours.

It is not uncommon in deliverance services to see Satan throw his victims around.

AN ANGEL OF LIGHT

2 Cor. 11:14. And no marvel; for Satan himself is transformed into an angel of light.

Satan is a deceiver. Walk holy before the Lord; be filled with divine love. Rid yourself of all critical spirits. Allow no room for hate or malice. Satan would like to get his foot into your life through one of these areas.

Often Satan comes as an angel of light. If the individual isn't spiritually minded, he will be thoroughly convinced that it is the Lord.

If you have lived a life of sin, or subjected yourself to cults, or if you have had a nervous breakdown, then you need to take much heed to these words. Satan will try to deceive you. Seek counsel with an understanding and wise person in the Lord Jesus Christ. Check out all visions, revelations, and voices.

If you have a very hard and dogmatic spirit about your revelations, more than likely you are ignorantly covering up for a demon spirit that is deceiving you.

One lady had a very weird prophetic utterance. I rebuked the devil. She was very much offended. Very harshly she declared that she knew that she was moving in the Holy Ghost. Later I found that she had tried to break up every good church in town with this spirit. She was so "ornery" and "mean" that she wasn't aware of how much Satan was using her.

Beware of abnormal attitudes in your heart, such as covetousness and greed. I know of a lady who was led to Jesus by a pastor. He taught her to move in the spirit but somehow he did not get the message of love into her heart. She secretly had a desire to be pastor of the church. This grew and grew. Finally her prophecies were infiltrated with this evil spirit. The pastor did not have the discernment to detect this at first. He began to yield to her prophecies. Soon he was completely demon possessed. He desired to take his own life. Needless to say, after he was delivered, this woman was pastoring his church.

There is no room in this walk for hard, stubborn, independent spirits. If you have these, you are entertaining evil spirits. Get on your face and repent. Change these attitudes. Stop yielding to them. Resist the devil until he flees from you. Reap the fruits of the spirit and practice yielding to them. Let the Christ nature come forth.

One of Satan's prime operations is to deceive. One minister was approached by a harsh voice which said, "I am God Almighty. From henceforth you will not preach in the name of Jesus. You will preach in the name of the Father and the Son and the Holy Ghost. You will go through a long period of sickness. You will then come into a great ministry. No one will believe you. You will be persecuted."

We will not discuss the name of Jesus here other than to quote Col. 3:17: "Whatsoever ye do in word or deed, do all in the name of the Lord Jesus, giving thanks to God and the Father by him." The scripture plainly teaches that there is no other name under heaven given to men whereby we may be saved. So this is plainly a deception.

Satan wants to be worshipped. He will tell any sort of a lie to get your devotion. Many times, in dealing directly with Satan, I have been forced to try the spirits according to 1 Jn. 4:1-3. He will declare that he is god. He will declare that somebody else is god but he will never declare that Jesus Christ is Lord or that Jesus Christ is come in the flesh.

It is apparent that Satan was deceiving this minister. He took a part truth and misapplied it. This is the same approach he used on Jesus in chapter four of Matthew.

SICKNESS

Job 2:7. So went Satan forth from the presence of the Lord, and smote Job with sore boils...
Acts 10:38. How God anointed Jesus of Nazareth with the Holy Ghost and with power: who went about doing good, and healing all that were oppressed of the devil...
Acts 19:12. So that from his body were brought unto the sick handkerchiefs or aprons, and the diseases departed from them, and the evil spirits went out of them.

Smith Wigglesworth, a successful deliverance minister of yesterday, would always cast out the demon of cancer when praying for people with cancer. Much of our sickness is just another manifestation of demonic forces at work. Jesus went about "healing all that were oppressed of the devil."

"Diseases departed from them, and the evil spirits went out..." Notice the close relationship between sickness and evil spirits. They seem to be working together. Diseases and evil spirits seem to be first cousins. Sickness is just a title for manifestations of spirits. Study closely their connections in the scriptures. Mt. 4:24 is a good place to begin. "They brought unto him all sick people that were taken with divers diseases, and torments, and those which were possessed with devils, and those which were lunatic, and he healed them all." Sick people here are described as those with divers diseases, torments, possessed with devils, and lunatics. We know torments would be evil spirits. Those possessed with devils would be a more complete manifestation of evil spirits. Lunatics were treated in the scripture as evil spirits. Mt. 17:15.

LYING SPIRITS

Gen. 3:4. And the serpent said unto the woman, Ye shall not surely die.
Jn. 8:44...He is a liar, and the father of it.
 Satan has always been a liar. There is a spirit of lying that may enter through a door left open to him.

 One man that I dealt with began to smoke on the side. He was hypocritical about it. He tried to deceive others. This was a lie. He soon began to lie to his customers. Soon he was dominated by a poverty spirit. He could not make money. Every way he turned he lost money. As he confessed these sins, Jesus set him free. Immediately things straightened out for him.

STIFFNESS

Lk. 13:16. Ought not his woman, being a daughter of Abraham, whom Satan hath bound, lo, these eighteen years, be loosed from this bond...
 Arthritis is a common form of stiffness. I have seen many people set free instantly by casting out this spirit.

Sometimes this spirit enters through the family line. Other times it could be a physical condition and not necessarily a spirit. In many cases, however, it is caused by attitudes such as a critical spirit, worry, hate, rebellion, etc.

One lady told me she had this disease all of her life. Upon questioning her I found out that her daddy hated her because she was a girl. She grew up being slapped around by her father. She developed a fear of and hate for her father. This opened her life to the spirit of arthritis.

Satan is back of all problems regardless of the immediate cause. He has caused the cause. Jesus will set the captives free today.

MIRACLES

Rev. 16:14. They are spirits of devils, working miracles...

Those who yield to spiritualism and such like have seen many miracles of Satan. Yet he is limited. The magicians' rods turned into serpents just like Moses' rod, but Moses' rod swallowed up the others.

Demon worshippers walk on hot coals without being burned, etc.

Many who are not wise in this day are being led off into false cults just for the supernatural kick. Man longs for the supernatural. It is time for God's children to walk into Canaan's land and come forth with the real supernatural power of the living God. Most people will never turn to the false when they have the real to enjoy.

Tables walking, bodies floating in the air

(levitation), voices talking, impersonation of the dead, etc., are very fascinating; however, this is a deception of Satan to divert your worship from the true God. The end of such people who follow this deception is problems upon problems in this life and eternal damnation.

Anyone really interested in knowing the truth about evil spirits can try the spirits. 1 Jn. 4:2-3, "...Every spirit that confesseth that Jesus Christ is come in the flesh is of God: And every spirit that confesseth not that Jesus Christ is come in the flesh is not of God: and this is that spirit of antichrist..." When talking to the evil spirit himself, he will never confess that Jesus Christ is come in the flesh. It is impossible for him to do so. However, sometimes the human spirit will respond instead of the evil spirit. The human spirit might confess that Jesus has come in the flesh. The best time to try the spirit is when he is manifesting himself strongly.

I have done this many, many times. One lady was thrown down in one of our services. I said, "Devil, has Jesus Christ come in the flesh?" She cried out, "No, He has not come in the flesh." Quickly the woman suppressed the spirit and said, "Oh, yes He did." She got up, brushed off her clothes, and left angrily. The next night she came back for deliverance. She was embarrassed that she could have an evil spirit.

DECEPTION

Rev. 12:9. ...Satan, which deceiveth the whole world...

Rev. 20:8. ...Shall go out to deceive the nations...

Rev. 20:10. The devil that deceived them...

Many people are deceived by satanic influences and do not know it.

How does Satan get a foothold in our lives to deceive us? He comes in through our mind generally. We begin to listen to him, as Eve did. As we entertain a harsh, mean, rebellious, hateful, covetous, or other attitude contrary to the fruits of the Spirit, we open the door to Satan. Some of these attitudes may be ever so slight at first, but soon they grow stronger and stronger without our fully realizing what is happening to us. The only cure is to be very tender and sensitive before the Lord.

Develop an attitude of childlikeness before the Lord. Many times we miss the Lord when new truths come along. If it is not in our flow of previously established teachings, according to our understanding, we have a tendency to reject it as false. Examine everything, but do not accept everything. Sometimes this takes weeks and months of searching before you begin to get the full picture. Learn to place things on the shelf if you do not understand them. That way you neither accept nor reject them. They are there to receive if you ever need them.

Too often people have everything figured out, and they are certain that they are correct. This is true of many folks with new revelations, also. A dogmatic spirit is usually not right. Apparently most of these folks are wrong in some areas because they all differ in opinions (many schools of thought on a given issue).

Walk softly before the Lord. Keep your heart open to flow with the Lamb whichever way He goes. If you have a dogmatic set of ideas on how things are to be in the end time, chances are you are deceived, also. The Word must be understood as the Spirit opens it to us. So be not deceived in this hour.

Some prayer groups are dominated by leaders who have problems at home or other places. In some cases it is a woman who is very rebellious against her husband. This mean, rebellious spirit soon begins to dominate the prayer group and others. It isn't long until they are caught up in the subtle deceiving spirit. This group may begin to manifest an exalted opinion of themselves. They may feel like they are the only ones who are right. They feel everyone hates them. They develop a persecution complex. They become very critical in some cases.

Another sign of this type of deception in a group is that they become clannish. They no longer have an outreach. They lose their concern for others. They are God's little elect group in their own deceived minds. Many of these prophesy and move in revelation ministries. Much of this is in the soulish realm or direct demonic revelations.

Some people or groups get deceived by false teachings. Books and tapes that use quotations from the Bible to teach contrary to the basic teachings of the Bible are deceptive. Some of these teachings are way out. They will talk about Jesus and Christ like fundamental believers. However, upon further inspection, you will find that they teach that Christ is in every man. They teach that Christ was just a good man like other great men. Many of those in this class teach that man is his own God. God may be out there somewhere, but basically man is a god unto himself, or his mind is his god. (Whatever he thinks will soon become a reality.) Some of these teachings are very close to the truth, but they are subtle. They glorify man rather than Jesus. They take a partial or near truth and apply it to pervert the real truth.

Christ is the Son of God who came from heaven. He was born of the virgin Mary. He is Lord. He is Savior. He is God. Man is lost until he personally accepts Jesus Christ as Lord.

A group that has been caught up in error like this is very difficult to reach. They are blinded by Satan. Some of these people start out as very sincere Christians. Their sincerity and simplicity grows less and less as they become more involved in this deceptive worship of Satan. Some have been heard to say, "I don't care what the Bible says, I will follow my own spirit revelation." Is. 8:20, '...If they speak not according to this word, it is because there is no light in them." If we are not basicaly in line with the Word of God, we are in Satanic deception. A denomination or church that holds to traditional church doctrine that conflicts with the Word of God is in demonic deception. Anything that separates you from the main workings of the Spirit and sets you up as some great one is satanic. Some of the new churches and groups are falling into this error. This is true of some of the old-line churches also.

Anything that has to be defended and pushed by fleshly attitudes is not of God. He can take care of Himself. A truth can be proclaimed and ministered; but as soon as you put your hand to it, you cause it to become perverted. Many great truths have been discovered in the Word of God. The moment flesh begins to defend them, they become pushed out of the realm that the Spirit meant for them to be. Many partial truths lie buried in error now because man put his hand to it.

Anytime your spirit becomes defensive then you are in a sectarian spirit. Your joy begins to drain. Many of your religious or church services become bound. Jesus is no longer the real center of worship. Other motives lie deep and secretly hidden within. As you go to worship the Lord, time after time you wonder why there is a binding upon the service. A deceptive spirit is working.

Many of our "so-called" divine order groups get so defensive and dogmatic that it is evident that a sectarian spirit has taken over. Other groups within the same fellowship are tender and loving and flow with Jesus. So make sure that the truth you have discovered has not become perverted in your fleshly hands by a deceptive spirit.

Chapter 8

MUCH OF JESUS' MINISTRY AND THAT OF THE NEW TESTAMENT CHURCH WAS SPENT IN CASTING OUT DEVILS

JESUS' MINISTRY

Mt. 4:24. His fame went throughout all Syria: and they brought unto him all sick people that were taken with divers diseases, and torments, and those which were possessed with devils, and those which were lunatic, and ... he healed them all.
Mt. 8:28...There met him two possessed with devils, coming out of the tombs, exceeding fierce, so that no man might pass by that way.
Mt. 8:16. When the even was come, they brought unto him many that were possessed with devils: and he cast out the spirits with his word, and healed all that were sick.
Lk. 13:16. Ought not this woman, being a daughter of Abraham, whom Satan hath bound, lo, these eighteen years, be loosed from this bond on the Sabbath day?

Many other places could be cited such as the girl grievously vexed with a devil in Mt. 15:22. Jesus set them all free. Not only did He do so but He commanded the twelve to do so in Lk. 9:1. He commanded the seventy to take dominion over devils in Lk. 10:19-20. He called every believer to this ministry in Mk. 16:17.

THE NEW TESTAMENT CHURCH MINISTRY

Acts 5:16. There came also a multitude out of the cities...bringing sick folks, and them which were vexed with unclean spirits: and they were healed every one.
Acts 8:7. For unclean spirits, crying with loud voice, came out of many that were possessed with them: and many taken with palsies, that were lame, were healed.
Acts 19:12. So that from his body were brought unto the sick handkerchiefs or aprons, and the diseases departed from them, and the evil spirits went out of them.

There are more needs today than ever before. The church is filled with spirits of oppression and depression. The average minister and believer is content to leave the Devil alone and put up with him. No wonder preachers are quitting the ministry. With these powers working within, nothing can run smoothly.

The world is filled with problems which are nothing but demon spirits taking over. Dope is just another demon. Alcohol is another demon. Sex perverts have been delivered in our services in Jesus' name.

The world needs our help. The church needs deliverance. Many of our so-called good men in the church will fight a real move of God when it hits the church. These men need deliverance.

Woe to the slothful minister in this day. Stop

turning a deaf ear to the needs of the flock. Arise now from your sleep of tradition and denominationalism, pentecostal preachers not excluded. They are among some of the worst about rejecting the real deliverance ministry.

Shake yourself from the dust of tradition and arise in the very ministry of Jesus Christ. Is. 52:12, "Awake, awake; put on thy strength...shake thyself from the dust; arise, and sit down...loose thyself from the bands of thy neck, O captive daughter of Zion." This is God's Word for you today. Break the bonds of your tradition and unbelief. Break the bondage of fear of man and your denomination. Shake yourself from the dust that has settled down on your thinking. Enter into your ministry right now.

To the Spirit-filled believers in Eph. 5:14 Paul said, "...Awake thou that sleepest, and arise from the dead..."

With Paul I say to you believers today: Wake up and stop dodging the issue.

Set the captives free.

Chapter 9

THE TRUTH SHALL SET YOU FREE

Jn. 8:32. And ye shall know the truth, and the truth shall make you free.

Rom. 10:8...The word is nigh thee, even in thy mouth, and in thy heart: that is the word of faith, which we preach.

Rom. 10:9-10. That if thou shalt confess with thy mouth the Lord Jesus, and shalt believe in thine heart that God hath raised him from the dead, thou shalt be saved. For with the heart man believeth unto righteousness; and with the mouth confession is made unto salvation.

Mt. 10:32. Whosoever therefore shall confess me before men, him will I confess also before my Father which is in heaven.

Mk. 11:23...He shall have whatsoever he saith.

Victory in the Christian life is based on identification with the Word of God. Jn. 8:32 declares: "The truth shall set you free." The opposite is true, also. Lies will bring you into bondage.

Rom. 10:8 tells us that as the Word of God is in our mouth and in our heart, then faith is built. Faith destroys the enemy's hold in our life. The truth really will set you free.

Rom. 10:9-10 is the foundation of deliverance. We confess it with our mouth and believe it in our heart. Deliverance immediately follows. Christianity is based on confession. Mt.

10:32 clearly teaches that as we confess Jesus here on earth, then He confesses us to the Father. This is not limited to initial salvation. It also includes deliverance from any form of demonic influence in your life. Mark 11:23 plainly states that we have what we will say.

Start now by identifying with your legal nature. Your legal nature is Jesus. Your old nature is Satan. This latter nature is the failure nature. It is the sick nature. It is the weak nature. It is the nervous nature. Get up out of this illegal nature and declare yourself to be of the new creation. You are a new person in Jesus Christ. Stop identifying with the illegal nature. Declare yourself to be free in Jesus Christ. Declare yourself to be full of divine health, strength, etc. Make a series of bold positive statements many times during the day such as: I am living in divine health. I am living in prosperity. I am living in peace. I am living in joy.

Study the fruits of the spirit in Gal. 5:22. They are love, joy, peace, longsuffering, gentleness, goodness, faith, meekness, and temperance.

If you are troubled with a hate spirit, repeat over and over during the day this statement: I am living in love for my fellow man.

It will be good and very powerful to get your companion, husband, wife, or other close friend, to agree with you. Confess it together several times a day.

Many times a day I make bold statements like these with my wife. As we are working in the house or traveling in our car, I will join hands with her in Jesus' name and say: Honey, we are living in prosperity. We are living in abundance.

We are living in peace and restfulness. We are longsuffering with each other and with our fellow man. We are gentle. We are walking in love and compassion.

If something happens that you don't live up to your confession, ask the Lord to forgive you immediately; laugh at the devil; and take authority over him. Return immediately to your confession.

You have spent years building error into your spirit. Now give the Word of God a chance to take firm root.

You can study your own life. Regardless of your problem, find a positive statement to come against it. You are now learning to walk in the truth which sets you free.

Just recently we were dealing with several demon possessed Christians. One girl said, "If you had not dealt with me tonight, I would have taken my life this very night."

The evil spirits kept speaking back to me. They would say, "We have this girl. She knows we have her. She is helpless. She has no hope. She is weak. She is a failure. I am going to kill her. This went on for three hours. Satan was ministering fear and unbelief to her. All the while I was ministering victory and strength and deliverance to her in Jesus' name.

Finally, I commanded her to speak in Jesus' name the following: "I am strong. I am more than a conqueror. I can do all things through Jesus Christ. I will live and not die. I am not afraid." Immediately she threw up her hands and began to sob and cry out of her heart to Jesus, constantly confessing victory and strength.

Satan left immediately without a sound. She kept praising the Lord. She was back the next day still delivered. This time she had another Christian who was bound like she had been.

Notice that Satan tried to build fear and doubt and unbelief through his words and thoughts. We built Christ into her through the living Word of God. God's Word is true. It is powerful. It is greater than demonic forces.

You stop identifying with what ministers fear, failure, and unbelief, and start confessing and thinking victory and strength. The moment you begin to identify with the truth you will be free.

Recently I was praying for a woman who was full of fear. This also was a born again believer. Satan would repeat over and over: "She is no good. We have been here too long. She knows I have her, etc." I would come against him with the Word of God. Soon I commanded her to repeat: "I am not afraid." She began to whimper like a dog, "I am afraid, I am afraid he will come back, I am afraid I can't hold out." She did this several times. Finally in the authority of Jesus Christ with a heart of love and compassion I said, "Shut that up and stop letting the devil minister to you. He is trying to defeat you. Get up on your feet and shout the victory." She began to identify with victory and instantly Satan left. Oh, what a glorious time she had loving the Lord following her deliverance. Hallelujah!

We have found that whether it is a complete demonic possession of certain areas of your life or just mild depressions of fear and negative attitudes, etc, you can be set free in Jesus' name by a positive attitude toward God's Word.

Further, we have discovered that these negative spirits that minister to all of us are Satan's ministers trying to get us to yield to him thousands of times daily.

My answer to you at this point is: Stop letting your life be infiltrated by demonic lies. Let God be true and every man or experience a liar.

As you learn to stand on the Word of God, then deliverance will come.

Sometime ago I found it difficult to sleep soundly at night. This had been working for years. I could sleep fairly well but not as a Christian should. I began to confess that I was filled with a loving attitude toward all areas of life, and that I was filled with peace and rest. What was I doing? I was identifying with the Word of God in regard to the fruits of the spirit. Within three days I was resting normally. Praise the Lord.

I have found that should deliverance be slow in coming, we must let God be true and every man a liar. Just keep on confessing. Deliverance is moving in. You have spent a life time rooting your life with Satanic thoughts. Now give the Word of God a chance to take root in you.

Satan cannot operate against your will. Your will is involved in victory. Your will is involved in your bondage. Recently I heard a medical doctor testify on the effect of one's will in relationship to deliverance. After counseling some of his patients that were beyond the reach of medicine, he would tell them to go home and command the infirmity to leave in Jesus' name. Many reported complete recovery at once. You do have authority. Whomever you yield to, his servant you will become. Set your will on God's Word. Refuse symptoms. Let God's Word prove itself strong in your behalf.

Books By Author

The Implanted Word $1.95
Discipleship Pro and Con 1.95
Setting the Captives Free 1.50
You Can Receive the Holy Ghost Today 1.25
The Pendulum Swings 1.50
The Laws of the Spirit 1.50
Deliverance From the Bondage of Fear 1.50
Favor, the Road to Success 1.25
Confession Pack (32 cards with related
    Scriptures on both sides) 1.00
Race Horse 1.25

All ten of the above for $10.50 plus postage.

When ordering up to three books include 50¢ postage. Add 5¢ postage for each additional book.

Texas residents please include 4% sales tax.

On orders of 30 books or more you may deduct 35%. This discount does not apply when ordering the set of 10 at the special set price.

Please add postage and sales tax on discounted totals if applicable.

Bob Buess, Box 959, Van, Texas 75790